T0198964

WHAT ARE DRUGS?

A Parent's Doorway to a Difficult Topic

LYNN FIELD

To order additional copies of this book, contact:
Xlibris
1-888-795-4274
www.Xlibris.com
Orders@Xlibris.com

Dedicated to

**Allan, Kaitlynn, Sommer-Rose and Blair- McKenzie.
In the hope their future does not include drugs.**

"What are drugs?"
I hear you ask.
To answer this
Is no simple task.
There are two types
Of drugs, you see.
One makes you better;
One brings misery.

Good drugs are legal.
The law says they're okay.
These drugs pass lots of tests
To keep it that way.
They include coffee and tobacco,
And cough mixture too.
As well as antibiotics
Prescribed just for you.

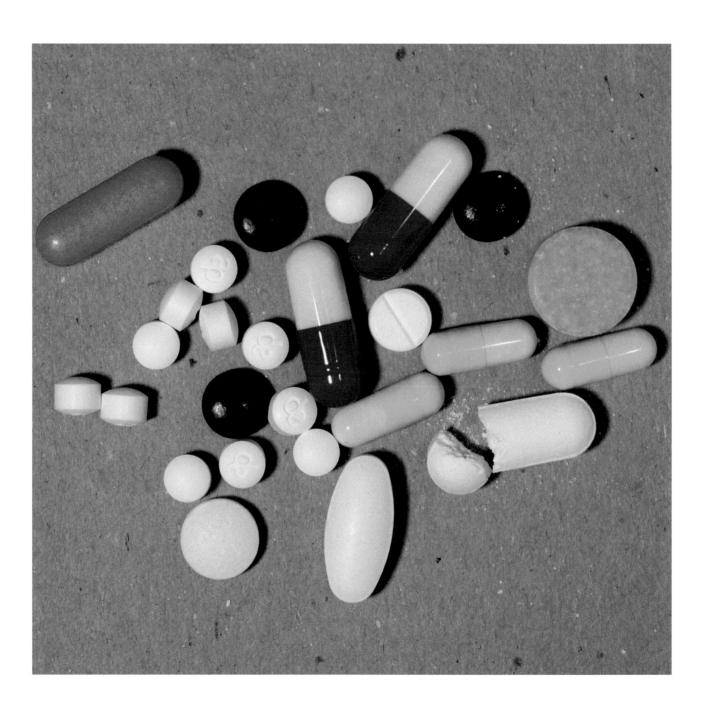

Any drug can hurt you
If you use too much.
Or take someone else's medicine,
Or mix good ones and such.
If you take prescribed drugs
As you're told to do,
These drugs won't hurt;
They will work for you.

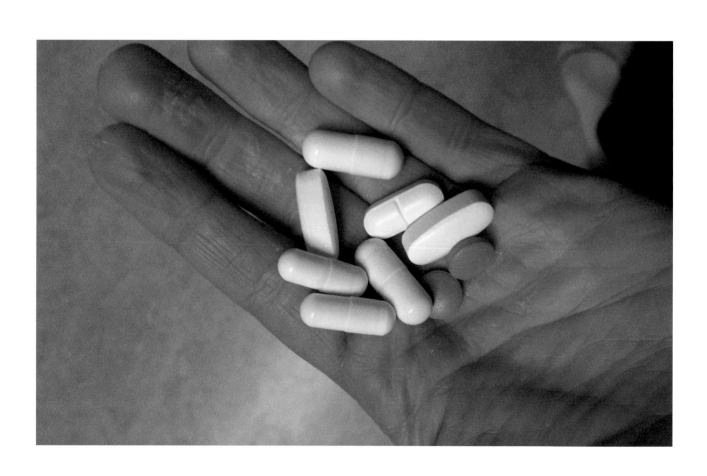

Bad drugs are taken
To forget some pain,
To block it out
So memories won't remain.
To make those who take them
Feel that they belong
In a world where they don't.
And that's where it is wrong.

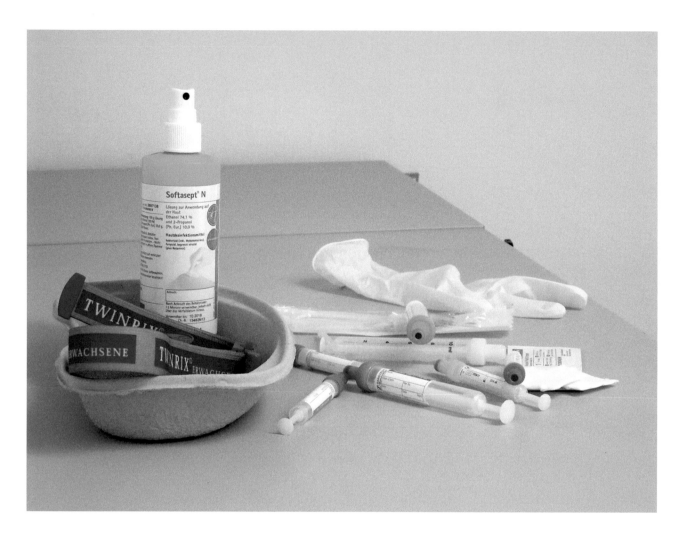

Drugs take much more
Than they ever give.
They take your family
And a chance to live.

They create secrets
And lies and fear.
They hurt the people
We hold most dear.
When people use drugs wrong,
Their bodies crave.
And only by not using them
Their lives they save.
Drugs affect your thoughts,
Your actions, your deeds.
Your only thought is for
The drug that you need.

Before you try a drug
Just for fun,
Consider the drug
A bullet in a gun.
Make sure you know
What you are taking.
The decision you make
Is the life that you're making.
Bad drugs have stuff in them,
Like toilet cleaner.
It makes you feel sick
And act a lot meaner.

It can shut down your body
And cloud your mind.
Reality is a memory
That's hard to find.

T+ - Très toxique

Some people call bad drugs their medicine
because they make them feel better.
They make them tired and sleepy
Instead of go-getters.
Bad drugs take their money,
So they don't have any feed.
There is nothing more important
Than the drug that they need.

Good Drugs, Bad Drugs

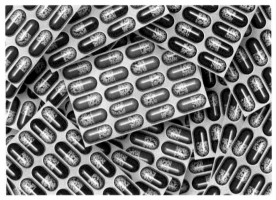

Good drugs are medicine.
They come in a box
Made by a chemist
And kept under locks.

They keep people well
And make them feel better.
They're prescribed by a doctor
In a special letter.

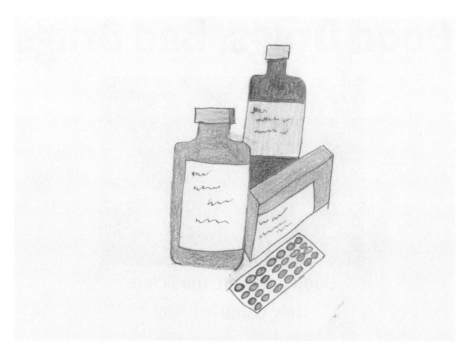

Good drugs are cough syrup,
Antibiotics, and creams.
They have medicines for everything;
At least so it seems.

Good drugs come with
Your name on the wrapping.
They are only for you,
So ill health you're lapping.

Bad drugs are different.
The doctor doesn't prescribe these.
The law says they're wrong, and
They're not aimed to please.

They don't make you feel better.
They make you misbehave.
You can't do what you want;
You are the drugs' slave.

There are many names
That make drugs sound cool.
But if you take bad drugs,
You're anyone's fool.

Bad drugs make you feel happy
And then make you feel sad.
They make you do things
You wish you never had.

Bad drugs give you chills.
They make you forget
The important things, like
Your family and pet.

Bad drugs make you feel sick,
Feel like life isn't worth living.
They trick you into believing that
Drugs are forgiving.

Bad drugs come in needles,
Or they come in pills.
You can smoke them or snort them.
Any enjoyment they kill.

Drugs can damage your brain,
Your kidneys, and heart.
The only way to avoid this
Is don't ever start.

Printed in the United States
By Bookmasters